All The Things I Should Have said...

A collection of poetry
By: p.m. fisher

Dedication

First, I'd like to thank God for guiding
me always and showing me that he will
help me get through anything. I'd like to
thank my family for showing endless
support in everything I do. Also thank
you to everyone else who has supported
me along this crazy journey. Thank you
to those who have shown me love when
I needed it. Thank you to those who
have hurt me, you forced me to become
the strongest I've ever been. Thank you
to those who came into my life and
didn't stay, and for the lessons that will
stay with me always.

Contents

Prologue

In the beginning I was afraid to share my work with others. I was hesitant to let others hear my inner thoughts and literary creations. I did not want to be judged. In time I learned to share my words. I have become more comfortable with my work and have accepted the risk. I have accepted the vulnerability because in this space I have created something beautiful. I am proud to be able to share my deepest emotions and feelings with you all.

Every beautiful moment ends
like the sun sets at night
like a candle burning out
driving fast to a red light
I wasn't ready to let this feeling go
do anything to keep you here
my vision is clouded
but I see clear

I don't know if it was the sparkle in your
eyes
or the way your lips touch mine
but I've fallen in love with you
every single time...

Your love shines on me
you give me life
like water to a flower
like the moon to the night

In another life
it's you & me
for now
we'll never be

I can't control my breathing
my heart races when we touch
it feels so natural like summer rain
kissing you alleviates the pain

When *like* turns into *love*
when *for now* turns into *forever*
when *you* turn into a place that feels like
home
that's when I knew

When I'm in pain
I find relief in your arms
never in any harm

My eyes were closed
but I saw who he truly was
as we lay in bed
he told me his dreams
the thoughts in his head

Just like a mosquito
I fall into your web
I try to avoid you
but you always pull me in

I water myself, then I water you
I give you half each time
when I come up short
I still give you more than mine
I keep watering & watering
hoping you'll grow
wishing you'd give me a little
wishing you'd know

Your skin is rich
your roots run deep
your hair full of curls
you talk in your sleep
you sing when no one's listening
I love to pay attention
I love to watch you compete
I love to listen to your thoughts
I love to hear about your dreams

Summer is gone
I'm starting to see
the lessons I've learned
the things you've failed to see
your high won't last forever
you will come down and you will know
who I truly was
who you didn't get to know
fall will come & fall will go
when winter begins
you will feel the snow...

I miss your touch
the way your skin feels against mine
how you would kiss me slowly
as if there is no such thing as time

People say they care
claim they miss you and are never there
where were you when I felt alone
would we even be speaking if I didn't pick up
the phone
it sucks always having to reach out
being the one who plans everything
people are selfish
they only call when they need something
they only reach out for information
it sucks that if I don't speak first
there won't be a conversation

You are a broken man
forced to work a 9 to 5
you do your best
but can barely survive

You make me feel sorry
taking advantage of my kind heart
fathers are supposed to protect you
not tear you apart

You looked in the mirror
more than you looked at me
in competition with your reflection
I'll never compete

Tired of boys
pretending to be men
convincing me otherwise
showing their true colors in the end

I ended things
that was just a statement
nothing really changes
you've been complacent
with giving barely half
never showing up
never holding it down
I gave up
I gave all I could
no regrets on my part
just the love that's left for you
lost in my heart

You're all the same
you let me go
then wish you stayed
then want me back
then give me away

I stopped asking
I stopped complaining
I knew you didn't
so, I stopped waiting
I stopped hoping
I understood what it was
I understood what we were
I gave up
as did you
I couldn't take it anymore
nor could you
the difference is
I let you go
I question how long you'd keep this up
if there was someone else
if I was enough?

If I have to repeat myself
time & time again
you heard me
you've just chosen not to listen

He threw me in the backseat
like I was baggage
would rather lose me
would rather leave me damaged...

In need of love
I call out your name
you come to me
but never stay
in need of affection
I settle for your attention
but it doesn't last long
neither do you
I never finish
but you always do

You feel, & feel, & feel
you trap yourself in a cage
your pain is real
you stay hidden, locked away
you won't let yourself heal
you won't let anyone in
you're scared they won't understand
please just let me in

It's the little things
the willingness to go out your way
to do what I ask
to hear what I say
to remember what I want
to do what makes me smile
even if you don't want to
it's the simplest gestures
that mean the most
I shouldn't have to tell you
you should just know...

You wear your smile like a band aid
it's okay to air it out
you don't always have to cover up
your scars are beautiful
don't ever be ashamed
you've come so far
don't ever change

The things...
that I'd do in a *heartbeat*,
that you *hesitate* to,
the fact that I'd do just about *anything*,
be *everything*,
for *you*.

You think you're the big dog now...
I think you forgot who got you out the dog
pound,
I think you forgot who use to take the check,
I think you forgot who use to have your back,
I think you forgot who use to pick you up
Now you're too busy to talk, too busy to care,
I don't have time for people who are never
there
when you end up back in the pound
don't expect me to be around
I gave you shelter, gave you a home
yet you're so busy to pick up a phone

The type of woman who gives two shits
about a man
the one who puts her kids first
the one who gives them all she can
the type of woman who has to be a father too
she's a true queen
came from the bottom
built her own throne
all on her own

The sweetest revenge
is the purest of its kind
you finally stop caring
now they can't get you out of their mind...

When life gets hard
you are supposed to fight
but you choose
to not see the light
only if you knew
the flower you could become
if you just push through

I cried
I prayed
I even wish we never met
But wounds heal
and we learn to forget
we learn to forgive
we learn to let go

Things are broken
to become new again
I had to fall apart
to fully comprehend
I had to lose myself
to find who I really am
I had to learn to love myself
before I let you in

I'm a wildfire
vibrant and free
she's but a mere flame
she'll never be me.

I texted
I called
and still no answers at all
I wrote letters
I was too afraid to send
I wrote poems you'll never comprehend
I talked about you all the time
till one day I realized
I probably never even cross your mind...

She'll never see how you look with tears in
your eyes
she'll never feel your love because you're
afraid to try
she'll never satisfy you because she isn't me
and I leave wounds you can never see

You'll go insane if you wonder what could
have been
you must take things as they are
you must see people for who they are
you must understand that not everything is
for you
you must just accept
accept failure
accept pain
accept disappointment
and eventually you will move on from this
something better will come
someone better will appear
what once hurt you
will disappear

Do not be mad for what you do not receive
for what he has given you
is all you need

When you get a cut
you don't go right away and pour salt all over
it
you wait
you let it dry, let it heal
wounds take time
the pain is real
don't go back to him
don't try to work it out
if he wanted you, he'd already have you back
because you love him
does he love you back?

I look back at the girl I use to be
the little girl with hopes & dreams
I wonder if I'm who she wanted to be
am I her?
is she me?

He didn't consider your feelings
he didn't make sure you were okay
so why even worry
why wait?

If it comes to a point
where it's between you and I...
I'm always going to choose me
I know my intentions
if you're blind
I can't make you see

Take your time
enjoy the now
have fun
be free
find yourself
find who you're meant to be

(To be continued...)

Printed in Great Britain
by Amazon

84034364R00031